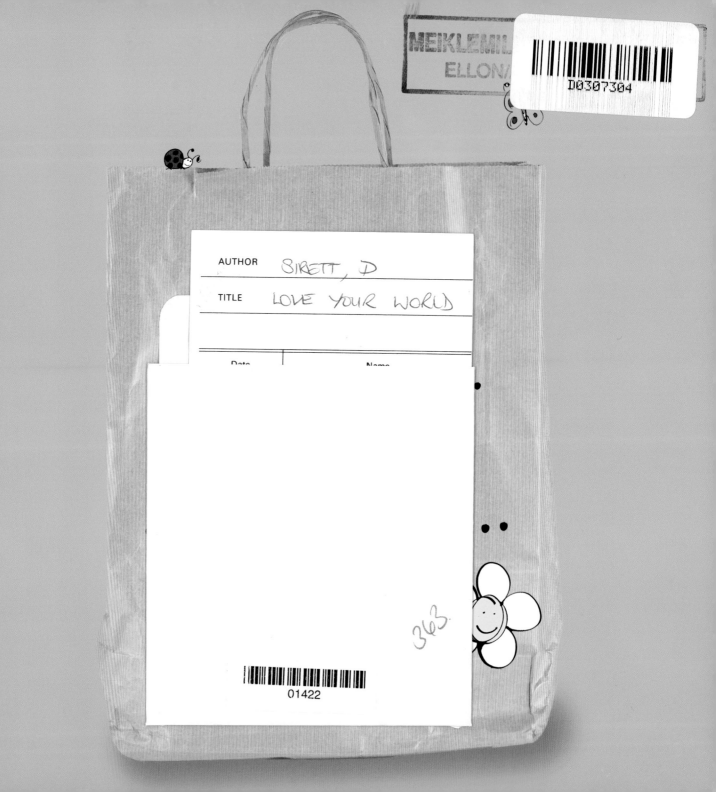

LONDON, NEW YORK,
MELBOURNE, MUNICH, AND DELHI

Written by Dawn Sirett
Designed by Rachael Parfitt and
Victoria Palastanga
Illustrations by Rachael Parfitt
Additional Design by Cathy Chesson
Special Photography by Howard Shooter and Dave King
Production Controller Lloyd Robertson
Production Editor Vivianne Ridgeway

With thanks to Will Heap for additional photography p9 bottom left, p21 full-page, and p32 top left.
And many thanks to Astrid and Olivia Bird, Phoebe Harrison, Louie Hunt, and Rex Palastanga
for their help making the beautiful recycled pictures, cards, and models, and to Sue Timpson
for making the wonderful papier mâché globe.

First published in Great Britain in 2009 by Dorling Kindersley Limited, 80 Strand, London WC2R 0RL

Copyright © 2009 Dorling Kindersley Limited
A Penguin Company

2 4 6 8 10 9 7 5 3 1
YD029 – 04/09

A CIP catalogue record for this book is available from the British Library.

ISBN: 978-1-40533-907-0

Printed and bound in Germany by Mohn Media

Mixed Sources
Product group from well-managed
forests and other controlled sources
www.fsc.org   Cert no. SA-COC-1592
© 1996 Forest Stewardship Council
FSC

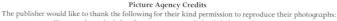

Picture Agency Credits
The publisher would like to thank the following for their kind permission to reproduce their photographs:
(Key: a=above; b=below/bottom; c=centre; f=far; l=left; r=right; t=top)
Alamy Images: Fotosonline / Klaus-Peter Wolf 6cb; Paul Kuroda 2tl (girl in barrel), 5crb, 34tl (girl in barrel),
35fcrb (girl in barrel); Robert Harding Picture Library Ltd / Ann & Steve Toon 6cl; Mark Ross 13cra; Igor Zhorov
2crb (bee), 4tl, 9tr, 34crb (bee), 35fclb (bee). **Corbis:** Ariel Skelley 6cra. **DK Images:** Jane Bull 2 (4 x plastic bag),
2bl (bucket), 2tr (bucket), 12bl, 12tl, 12tr, 16tl, 30crb (bucket), 30fclb (bucket), 32bc, 34 (4 x plastic bag), 34fbl
(bucket), 34tr (bucket), 35 (6 x plastic bag), 35bl (bucket). **Getty Images:** Iconica / Angelo Cavalli 16bl;
Photographer's Choice RR / Andrew Errington 25bl; Riser / Siri Stafford 2fbl (children), 25br, 31fbl (children),
34fbl (children); Stone / Frank Krahmer 2tr (tree), 8, 34tr (tree); Taxi / Simone Mueller 25tl. Photolibrary: 2cl
(butterfly), 5clb, 5cra, 9tl, 34cl (butterfly), 35bl (butterfly), 35tr (birdhouse); Digital Vision 5cla, 35cla
(big leaf). **Jacket images:** *Front:* **Alamy Images:** Paul Kuroda crb. **Photolibrary:** clb, cra; Digital Vision cla.
All other images © Dorling Kindersley. For further information see: www.dkimages.com

Discover more at
www.dk.com

love your world

how to take care of the plants, the animals, and the planet

DK

A Dorling Kindersley Book

Let's love our world and try each day,
To do all things the **GREENER WAY!**

Love the animals.

Love the people.

Love the plants.

Let's look after
all the things
in our world.

We're the
GREEN TEAM!

Let's make our planet perfect, too,
For wildlife and for me and you.

We could put a nesting box or a bird feeder in the garden...

...grow plants that bees and butterflies like...

ribbit! ribbit!

...and help make safe, green places for wildlife.

Let's fill a tray with soil...

I like soil!

...plant some seeds...

We'll grow a garden
In a tray,
So snails and worms
Will come and stay.

...make a stone path.

I'll live there!

...and add a yogurt-pot pond.

We can recycle
plastic, glass...

We won't
Waste things.
We'll all make sure
That we **RECYCLE**
More and more.

...foil, cans,
and tins.

...paper,
cardboard...

Let's give our old
clothes to jumble
sales, and buy
jumble, too!

We can
squash boxes
and recycle
them.

We can give old toys to charity and buy second-hand instead of new.

Let's think of all the things we can recycle where we live!

Good shot!

And to show
The world
How much we care,
We won't
Leave litter
ANYWHERE!

Let's put litter in the bin.

Or better still, **RECYCLE IT!**

And we'll **REDUCE**. That's super green!
Using less is what we mean.

...we'll use just **ONE BAG**, again and again!

We won't use loads of throw-away bags...

Instead of putting tons of packaging in the bin...

...we'll choose food with packaging we can **RECYCLE**.

And we won't run the tap while we brush our teeth. We'll turn it **OFF** and save water!

brush, brush, brush, **tap OFF!**

Having a shower instead of a bath saves water, too!

And, of course,
We won't forget
To make our homes
The greenest yet!

Let's save
energy around
the house!

Let's help
the grown-ups
go **GREEN!**

We'll put on our jumpers so the grown-ups
can turn the heating **DOWN!**

We'll ask the grown-ups
to switch the lights...

...**OFF** when we
leave a room.

I was a **tin**.
Now I'm a
pencil holder!

I was **scrap paper**.
Now I'm a **boat!**

And where we can,
We won't just lose it.
We'll try our best
To **REUSE IT!**

I was an **old sock**.
Now I'm a **puppet!**

I was a **newspaper**.
Now I'm **wrapping paper!**

This was a yogurt pot.
Now it's a plant pot!

Or we'll turn it into art.
We're wonderful and really smart!

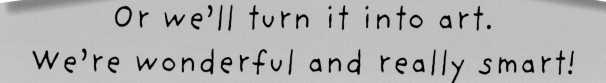

Let's use our imaginations!

We could make lovely cards and pictures from
scrap cardboard, paper, and stuff!

Or build amazing models...

zonk! zonk!

...with boxes, tubes, plastic bottles,
and any bits and bobs!

oink!
oink!

What shall
we make?

And each
One of us
Will get
A star...

We'll cycle...

...walk...

...when we go
without our car.

...scoot...

...or run!

And if we can, we'll all fly less.
We'll give the busy planes a rest!

Planes use lots of fuel and energy.

Let's try a
holiday nearer
to home!

brrm! brrm!

Sometimes we have to fly,
but if we're not going far,
we can take the coach or train.
That's much **GREENER!**

We don't
need to go far
to have a lovely time!

choo! choo!

And when all of these things we do,
We save the planet, me and you!

We've helped take care of
the people, the animals, the plants,
and the whole wide world!

We're all SUPER GREEN STARS!

I promise to:

Take care of my world.

Look after plants and animals.

Grow things.

Recycle things.

Never drop litter.

Give to, and shop at, jumble sales.

Reuse bags and choose things with less packaging.

Turn the tap off when I brush my teeth.

Ask the grown-ups to switch things off and turn the heating down.

Reuse things.

Turn things into art.

Walk, cycle, skate, or scoot more, and go by car less.

Tell people that coaches and trains are greener than planes!

Let's keep
Our green promises
Every day,
And be **SUPER GREEN,**
Hip hip hooray!

SUPER GREEN STAR
AWARD

THIS IS TO CERTIFY THAT .... HAS:

Helped to look after plants and animals

Recycled things

Reused things

Put litter in the bin

Turned the tap off when brushing teeth

Helped save energy around the house

Walked and cycled more, and travelled by car less

AND IS THEREFORE JUDGED TO BE:

A SUPER GREEN STAR!

SIGNED...

Cut along this line.